D0612188

THE ULTIMATE
NEW YORK GIANTS
TRIVIA BOOK

A Collection of Amazing Trivia Quizzes
and Fun Facts for Die-Hard Giants Fans!

Ray Walker

ISBN: 978-1-953563-98-9

Copyright © 2020 by HRP House

ALL RIGHTS RESERVED

No part of this book may be reproduced, stored in a retrieval
system, or transmitted in any form or by any means, electronic,
mechanical, photocopying, recording, scanning, or otherwise,
without the prior written permission of the publisher.

Exclusive Free Book

Crazy Sports Stories

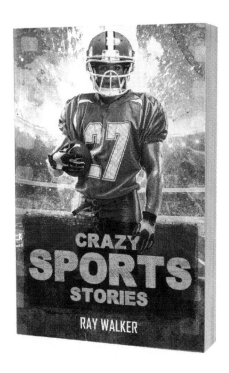

As a thank you for getting a copy of this book I would like to offer you a free copy of my book Crazy Sports Stories which comes packed with interesting stories from your favorite sports such as Football, Hockey, Baseball, Basketball and more.

Grab your free copy over at
RayWalkerMedia.com/Bonus

CONTENTS

Introduction 1

Chapter 1: Origins & History 3

Quiz Time! 3

Quiz Answers 8

Did You Know? 9

Chapter 2: Jerseys & Numbers 12

Quiz Time! 12

Quiz Answers 17

Did You Know? 18

Chapter 3: Giants Quarterbacks 21

Quiz Time! 21

Quiz Answers 27

Did You Know? 28

Chapter 4: The Pass Catchers 31

Quiz Time! 31

Quiz Answers 37

Did You Know? 38

Chapter 5: Running Wild **41**

Quiz Time! 41

Quiz Answers 47

Did You Know 48

Chapter 6: In the Trenches **51**

Quiz Time! 51

Quiz Answers 57

Did You Know? 58

Chapter 7: The Back Seven **61**

Quiz Time! 61

Quiz Answers 67

Did You Know? 68

Chapter 8: Odds & Ends & Awards **71**

Quiz Time! 71

Quiz Answers 77

Did You Know? 78

Chapter 9: Nicknames **81**

Quiz Time! 81

Quiz Answers 86

Did You Know? 87

Chapter 10: Alma Maters 90

Quiz Time! 90

Quiz Answers 96

Did You Know? 97

Chapter 11: In the Draft Room 100

Quiz Time! 100

Quiz Answers 106

Did You Know? 107

Chapter 12: The Trading Post 110

Quiz Time! 110

Quiz Answers 116

Did You Know? 117

Chapter 13: Super Bowl Special 120

Quiz Time! 120

Quiz Answers 126

Did You Know? 127

Conclusion 130

INTRODUCTION

The quest for another Super Bowl title has begun in New York and a talent-laden roster has Giants' fans excited about the direction of the franchise. With a storied history and a passionate fan base, expectations are running high as Saquon Barkley & Co. embark on their championship journey.

The Giants have rebuilt their roster and added a surplus of young, dynamic players who are ready to take the next step to become Super Bowl contenders. The G-Men and their loyal fanatics are poised and primed to return to the glory days of being one of the NFL's most successful clubs.

This fun and interesting book celebrates the players and coaches who have made key contributions to the growth of the franchise. From their early days in the 1920s to their Super Bowl runs in the 1980s, 1990s and 2000s, the Giants have become one of the most decorated franchises in NFL history.

Each chapter of this book features an exciting quiz with multiple-choice and true-or-false trivia questions. An answer key can be found on a separate page and there's also a section featuring 10 provocative "Did You Know? " facts about some of your favorite Giants.

Whether you use this book to test your knowledge of team history or to impress your family and friends, it will provide Giants fans with endless hours of entertainment.

Finally, the statistics and information in this book are current up to the beginning of 2020. So what are you waiting for? Find out how much Giants' history you really know and have fun at the same time!

CHAPTER 1:

ORIGINS & HISTORY

QUIZ TIME!

1. In which year was the New York Giants football team founded?

   a. 1920

   b. 1922

   c. 1925

   d. 1929

2. The Giants were one of five franchises that joined the NFL in 1925 and are the only one of that group still in existence today.

   a. True

   b. False

3. When Tim Mara founded the Giants, how much was his initial investment?

   a. $100

   b. $300

   c. $500

   d. $800

4. How many seasons did the Giants play their home games at the Polo Grounds?

    a. 27
    b. 31
    c. 35
    d. 40

5. Where was the first Giants preseason training camp held?

    a. Hoboken, New Jersey
    b. Princeton, New Jersey
    c. Morristown, New Jersey
    d. Pompton Lakes, New Jersey

6. The Philadelphia Eagles are the Giants' oldest rival in the NFC East. In which year did this storied rivalry begin?

    a. 1925
    b. 1930
    c. 1933
    d. 1935

7. The Giants play their home games at MetLife Stadium located at the Meadowlands Sports Complex in New Jersey, which they share with the New York Jets.

    a. True
    b. False

8. In 1966, the Giants lost to the Washington Redskins at DC Stadium in the highest-scoring game in league history. What was the final score of that game?

    a. 77-0
    b. 72-41

c. 70-35

d. 77-56

9. The Giants played their first exhibition game on October 4, 1925, in Connecticut. Which team did the Giants defeat 26-0 in their inaugural contest?

   a. Hammond Pros
   b. Buffalo Bisons
   c. Dayton Triangles
   d. All New Britain

10. Who was the first head coach in the history of the New York Giants football franchise?

    a. Tex Grigg
    b. Carl Storck
    c. Bob Folwell
    d. Scotty Bierce

11. New York used a ferocious defense in 1927 to finish with an 11-1-1 record and win their first NFL title. How many points did the Giants defense allow in 13 games?

    a. 20
    b. 22
    c. 26
    d. 29

12. The Giants won the first 12 games of their 1990 season, setting a record for the best start in the team's history.

    a. True
    b. False

13. New York set a franchise record for fewest turnovers in 1990 and finished the regular season with a 13–3 record. How many turnovers did the Giants have in 16 games?

    a. 10
    b. 12
    c. 13
    d. 14

14. In 2007, the Giants became the third NFL franchise to win 600 games in 2007. Which team did New York defeat on Monday Night Football for its 600th win?

    a. New York Jets
    b. Dallas Cowboys
    c. Atlanta Falcons
    d. Philadelphia Eagles

15. New York moved from Giants Stadium to what is now known MetLife Stadium in 2010. What was the name of MetLife Stadium at that time?

    a. New Jersey Stadium
    b. Meadowlands Stadium
    c. East Rutherford Stadium
    d. New Meadowlands Stadium

16. As of 2020, the Giants have the second-most enshrined members in the Pro Football Hall of Fame. How many former players and executives have been inducted into the Hall of Fame?

    a. 26
    b. 29

c. 31

d. 34

17. New York Giants' owner Tim Mara purchased the entire squad of the Detroit Wolverines in 1928 to acquire standout quarterback Benny Friedman.

a. True

b. False

18. The Giants hired a general manager who wasn't part of the ownership group for the first time in franchise history following the 1978 season. What was the name of New York's first general manager?

a. Bill Polian

b. Bob Ferguson

c. George Young

d. George Sauer Sr.

19. During Week 12 of the 1925 season, the Chicago Bears and their star player Red Grange visited the Polo Grounds to play the Giants. How many fans attended the game?

a. 40,000 to 45,000

b. 70,000 to 75,000

c. 60,000 to 65,000

d. 50,000 to 55,000

20. The Giants allowed more than 500 points on defense and finished the 1966 season with a league-worst 1–12–1 record.

a. True

b. False

QUIZ ANSWERS

1. C - 1925

2. A - True

3. C - $500

4. B - 31

5. D - Pompton Lakes, New Jersey

6. C - 1933

7. A - True

8. B - 72-41

9. D - All New Britain

10. C - Bob Folwell

11. A - 20

12. B - False (10 wins)

13. D - 14

14. C - Atlanta Falcons

15. D - New Meadowlands Stadium

16. B - 29

17. A - True

18. C - George Young

19. B - 70,000 to 75,000

20. A – True

DID YOU KNOW?

1. The Giants were incorporated in 1929 as the "New York National League Football Company, Inc." because New York had a professional baseball team with the same name. The franchise changed its legal corporate name in 1937 to "New York Football Giants, Inc."

2. Legendary Notre Dame football coach Knute Rockne coached his last game ever against the New York Giants in 1930. Rockne led a team of Notre Dame All-Stars in an exhibition game against the Giants at the Polo Grounds to raise money for unemployed people in New York. He was killed in a plane crash three months later while he was traveling to participate in the production of the film, *The Spirit of Notre Dame.*

3. Chicago Bears' owner George Halas nicknamed the Wilson football used in NFL games before the AFL merger "The Duke" after future Giants owner Wellington Mara, who was called "Duke" by Giants players because he was named after the Duke of Wellington. Halas named the ball after Tim Mara's son to reward the Giants founder for handling the contract that made Wilson the official supplier of footballs to the NFL. The league has used a newer version of "The Duke" in NFL games since 2006.

4. The 1956 Giants team that trounced the Chicago Bears 47-7 in the NFL title game had two future Hall of Fame coaches

on the sidelines. Tom Landry was at the helm of the defense for head coach Jim Lee Howell, while Vince Lombardi was calling the shots for the offense.

5. The Giants have often played spoilers by knocking off powerful teams with winning streaks. In 1998, the G-Men shocked the reigning Super Bowl champion Denver Broncos, who entered the game with a perfect 13-0 record. A decade later, the Giants ended the New England Patriots bid for an undefeated season with an upset in Super Bowl XLII. And, in 2011, New York snapped the Patriots 20-game home winning streak.

6. New York running back/defensive back Hank Soar was part of history in 1941 after getting into a fight with Green Bay Packer quarterback Larry Craig. Both Soar and Craig were fined $25 by NFL Commissioner Elmer Layden to become the first two players ever to be fined by the NFL's league office.

7. Aside from a short stint in the military during World War II, Giants co-owner Wellington Mara was involved with the Giants for more than 70 years. He started out as a ball boy in 1925 and spent his whole adult life with the franchise. He was inducted in the Pro Football Hall of Fame in 1997.

8. Giants head coach Tom Coughlin, along with NFL coaches Bill Cowher, Jeff Fisher, John Harbaugh and Jon Gruden resided at one of Saddam Hussein's former palaces in 2009 during a USO–NFL coaches' tour to Iraq.

9. Hall of Fame offensive tackle Steve Owen was hired by the Giants as a player-head coach in 1931 on a handshake deal. The Oklahoma native directed the team for the next 23 years despite never signing a contract. He guided the Giants to a pair of NFL championships.

10. The Giants and the Detroit Lions made history in a 1943 game even though neither team scored a single point. The game ended in a scoreless deadlock and no other NFL game has ever ended in a scoreless tie since then.

CHAPTER 2:

JERSEYS & NUMBERS

QUIZ TIME!

1. What was one of the Giants' primary color for the majority of their first 31 years that has slowly faded into the background?

   a. Gray

   b. Red

   c. White

   d. Blue

2. The Giants and the Pittsburgh Steelers are the only two teams in the NFL to have the players' uniform numbers on both the front and back of the helmets.

   a. True

   b. False

3. Tackle Art Lewis was the first draft pick in the history of the Giants. Which jersey number did he wear?

   a. 41

   b. 39

c. 23

d. 60

4. How many years did Hall-of-Famer Mel Hein wear number 7 for the Giants?

   a. 12

   b. 13

   c. 14

   d. 15

5. Tackle Steve Owen wore the most jersey numbers in franchise history. How many numbers did he wear?

   a. Six

   b. Four

   c. Five

   d. Three

6. The Giants signed fullback Larry Csonka as a free agent in 1976. Which player did he take No. 39 from?

   a. Bob Tucker

   b. Clyde Powers

   c. Bill Bryant

   d. Larry Watkins

7. When cornerback Dominique Rodgers-Cromartie switched to jersey No. 41 in 2015, it was his fifth different number in his career.

   a. True

   b. False

8. What was the nickname of the helmet the Giants introduced in 1933 that featured a blue shell with eight red stripes covering the crown?

   a. Spider Webs
   b. Zebra Stripes
   c. Spider Stripes
   d. Tiger Stripes

9. Which Giants player had his jersey retired due to making the ultimate sacrifice in WWII?

   a. Carl Grate
   b. Ray Poole
   c. Merle Hapes
   d. Al Blozis

10. What number did Hall-of-Famer Frank Gifford wear?

    a. 14
    b. 16
    c. 17
    d. 19

11. Which of the following logos was the Giants' official logo before the 1961 campaign?

    a. ny
    b. giants
    c. Giant Quarterback
    d. GIANTS

12. Besides Hall of Fame end Ray Flaherty, the only other player to wear No. 1 for the Giants was Frank Cope.

a. True

b. False

13. Although he wore No. 76 throughout his entire rookie season, Ereck Flowers decided to switch to his college number following the departure of teammate Geoff Schwartz. Which number did he switch to?

a. 70

b. 71

c. 73

d. 74

14. In which year did the Giants replace their red jersey with a white jersey with blue block numbers and no sleeve trim?

a. 1949

b. 1954

c. 1956

d. 1958

15. How many Giants quarterbacks have had their numbers retired?

a. 5

b. 3

c. 4

d. 6

16. Which number did Jim Thorpe wear during his lone season with the Giants in 1925?

a. 21

b. 22

c. 25

d. 28

17. Lawrence Taylor wore No. 55 during his first NFL game before switching to number 56 in his second contest.

    a. True

    b. False

18. Which two Giants players had No. 14 retired in their honor?

    a. Tuffy Leemans and Ward Cuff

    b. Ward Cuff and Y.A. Tittle

    c. Y.A. Tittle and Ken Strong

    d. Ken Strong and Tuffy Leemans

19. Safety Michael Johnson was a seventh-round draft choice by the Giants in 2007 and wore No. 43. What number did he switch to in 2008?

    a. 37

    b. 31

    c. 27

    d. 20

20. The Giants debuted a khaki belt with their uniform pants in 1960 but the belt lasted only one season.

    a. True

    b. False

QUIZ ANSWERS

1. B - Red

2. A - True

3. C - 23

4. D - 15

5. A - Six (6,12,36,44,50,55)

6. B - Clyde Powers

7. A - True

8. C - Spider Stripes

9. D - Al Blozis (#32)

10. B - 16

11. C - Giant Quarterback

12. B - False

13. D - 74

14. B - 1954

15. C - 4 (C. Conerly, Y.A. Tittle, P. Simms, E. Manning)

16. A - 21

17. B - False

18. B - Ward Cuff and Y.A. Tittle

19. D - 20

20. A – True

DID YOU KNOW?

1. Besides their home blue jerseys and road white jerseys, the Giants also had a third jersey. In a nod to their home red jerseys in the 1950s, New York had an alternate red jersey with white block numbers. However, these red jerseys were used in just four games before being retired in 2009. The Giants wore these alternate jerseys once against the Philadelphia Eagles (2004) and three times against the Dallas Cowboys (2005, 2006 and 2007).

2. The first player to have his number retired by the Giants was Hall of Fame end Ray Flaherty. When New York retired No. 1 in 1935, it was the first time any professional sports team in the United States had retired a jersey number.

3. The Giants debuted a new red helmet in 1930 to replace the brown helmets that were worn during the 1929 season. These new helmets featured a cross pattern on the crown and a blue bumper on the front.

4. The Giants ushered in a new era in 1961 and featured a logo on their helmet for the first time in team history. The franchise debuted a white lower-case "ny" logo on the sides of their blue helmet. The Giants won three consecutive NFL Eastern Division titles wearing this new logo.

5. Wide receiver Amani Toomer wore No. 89 during his first two years with the Giants but switched to No. 81 after the

1997 season because he simply "didn't like it." A member of the New York Giants Ring of Honor, Toomer felt strongly that a jersey number should feel as comfortable as a good pair of shoes.

6. When the Giants opened their new stadium in East Rutherford, New Jersey in 1976, the franchise introduced a new team logo for their helmet. The design was an italicized and underlined "GIANTS" in white letters.

7. The No. 14 has been retired twice by the Giants for two different players. The team originally retired the number in 1945 for halfback-wingback Ward Cuff. However, future Hall of Fame quarterback Y.A. Tittle asked for the number after New York acquired him in a 1961 trade. Tittle enjoyed great success with the Giants and the jersey was retired a final time in 1965.

8. The Giants' uniform jersey underwent drastic changes in 1975 when the club abandoned its traditional look for a more contemporary style. The blue jerseys had white numbers with red trim and featured sleeves with a five-stripe pattern -- two broad white stripes flanked by three thin red stripes.

9. A new-look helmet was also introduced in 1975. The player's numbers were no longer on the helmets and two thin white stripes were added to flank the helmet's red stripe. The traditional gray facemask was replaced with a white facemask.

10. In 2000, New York introduced a new modern look for their

uniform jerseys. The blue jerseys featured solid white numbers with no trim or striping and the "TV numbers" were positioned on the shoulders. The white jerseys were adorned with red numbers with blue trim instead of the previous blue numbers.

CHAPTER 3:

GIANTS QUARTERBACKS

QUIZ TIME!

1. Which Hall of Fame quarterback did the Giants acquire from the Minnesota Vikings (they traded him back to the Vikings five years later)?

   a. Earl Morrall

   b. Fran Tarkenton

   c. Craig Morton

   d. Y.A. Tittle

2. The Giants' loss to the Chicago Bears in the 1963 NFL Championship Game was their fifth defeat in the title game in six years.

   a. True

   b. False

3. Phil Simms was demoted to third-string quarterback in 1983. Which two quarterbacks were promoted by the Giants?

   a. Dave Brown and Kent Graham

   b. Jeff Hostetler and Mike Busch

c. Joe Pisarcik and Randy Dean

d. Scott Brunner and Jeff Rutledge

4. Which free-agent quarterback guided the Giants to Super Bowl XXXV after being signed as a free agent the previous season?

a. Dave Brown

b. Kurt Warner

c. Kerry Collins

d. Danny Kanell

5. Which one of the following quarterbacks did the Giants draft with their first pick in the 2004 NFL Draft?

a. Eli Manning

b. Philip Rivers

c. Phil Simms

d. Jeff Hostetler

6. What type of car was Giants quarterback Kyle Lauletta driving when he was pulled over and arrested for eluding police in 2018?

a. Hummer

b. Porsche

c. Ferrari

d. Jaguar

7. The Giants posted a 14-2 record in 1986, which was their best regular-season record since the NFL began playing a 16-game schedule in 1978.

a. True

b. False

8. Which CBS television series did Phil Simms make a cameo appearance in 2014 as a consultant in the art of knife throwing?

   a. *Criminal Minds*
   b. *Blue Bloods*
   c. *Elementary*
   d. *The Mentalist*

9. Which former University of Michigan All-American quarterback led the Giants to an 11-3 record in 1933 and set an NFL record at the time with 973 passing yards?

   a. Hap Moran
   b. Harry Newman
   c. Jack McBride
   d. Benny Friedman

10. Which Giants quarterback was sacked by Washington Redskins defensive end Bruce Smith for his 199th career sack, which set an NFL record for most sacks in league history?

    a. Phil Simms
    b. Kurt Warner
    c. Kerry Collins
    d. Jesse Palmer

11. Which Hall of Fame quarterback did Eli Manning replace during the 2004 season?

    a. Phil Simms
    b. Kerry Collins

c. Kurt Warner

d. Fran Tarkenton

12. Backup signal-caller Ryan Nassib was 5-for-5 for 68 yards and one touchdown in a lopsided loss to the Minnesota Vikings in 2015 and finished with a perfect 158.3 passer rating.

a. True

b. False

13. Which of the following quarterbacks was the first Giant to pass for 4,000 yards in a single season?

a. Dave Brown

b. Phil Simms

c. Craig Morton

d. Fran Tarkenton

14. Which journeyman quarterback, who was acquired in the trade for Fran Tarkenton, had his best season in 1972, when he led the league in completion percentage?

a. Earl Morrall

b. Gary Wood

c. Joe Pisarcik

d. Norm Snead

15. What type of medical condition in his throwing arm caused 1953 second-round pick Eddie Crowder to decline a contract with the Giants?

a. Nerve problem

b. Rotator cuff

c. Wrist tendonitis

d. Tennis elbow

16. In 2001, Kerry Collins set a single-season NFL record at the time for most fumbles. How many fumbles did he have that season?

    a. 20

    b. 21

    c. 23

    d. 27

17. Daniel Jones was the first quarterback in the Giants' history to begin his career with two wins as a starting quarterback for the franchise.

    a. True

    b. False

18. Which future teammate did Phil Simms finish runner-up to for the 1979 Rookie of the Year award?

    a. Rob Carpenter

    b. Leon Bright

    c. Johnny Perkins

    d. Ottis Anderson

19. How many consecutive games did Eli Manning start for the Giants from 2004 to 2017?

    a. 198

    b. 207

    c. 210

    d. 217

20. Kent Graham led the Giants to an upset win over the undefeated and reigning Super Bowl champion Denver Broncos, who went on to win their second consecutive title in Super Bowl XXXIII.

a. True
b. False

QUIZ ANSWERS

1. B - Fran Tarkenton

2. A - True

3. D - Scott Brunner and Jeff Rutledge

4. C - Kerry Collins

5. B - Philip Rivers

6. D - Jaguar

7. A - True

8. C - Elementary

9. B - Harry Newman

10. D - Jesse Palmer

11. C - Kurt Warner

12. A - True

13. B - Phil Simms

14. D - Norm Snead

15. A - Nerve Problem

16. C - 23

17. B - False (3rd, P. Simms and T. Tidwell)

18. D - Ottis Anderson

19. C - 210

20. A – True

DID YOU KNOW?

1. Former Giants quarterback Charlie Conerly was featured as the iconic "Marlboro Man" in commercials and billboards. The 1948 NFL Rookie of the Year, Conerly was a prolific passer who led New York to a lopsided victory over the Chicago Bears in the 1956 NFL Championship Game

2. Y.A. Tittle was considered a washed-up 34-year-old quarterback in 1961 when the Giants traded second-year guard Lou Cordileone to the 49ers for the future Hall-of-Famer. However, Tittle tossed a total of 69 touchdown passes during the 1962 and 1963 seasons and won back-to-back *Sporting News* NFL Player of the Year awards.

3. Daniel Jones, their first-round pick in 2019, became the first Giants' rookie quarterback to win his first career start since Scott Brunner in 1980. He also set an NFL record as the first rookie quarterback to have three games with 4 touchdown passes and no interceptions.

4. New York drafted a former Olympic handball player in the fifth round of the 1977 NFL Draft. Quarterback Randy Dean, whose highlight as a Giant was a one-yard touchdown pass, competed with his brother on the United States team that finished 10th at the 1976 Summer Olympics. He scored 24 goals in five matches for Team USA.

5. Bobby Clatterbuck started only two games in four seasons while serving as the Giants' backup signal-caller. However, he is most remembered for a game in which he was not the starting quarterback. The 316th pick in the 1954 NFL Draft, Clatterbuck wore glasses or contact lenses due to his poor eyesight. He was called into a game unexpectedly against the Cleveland Browns during his rookie season and entered the game without his contact lenses and had to throw "blind" to his receivers. Although he managed to put his lenses in during halftime, the Browns defeated the Giants in a low-scoring game.

6. Jeff Hostetler attained legendary status at the University of West Virginia after leading the Mountaineers to a pair of bowl games and 18 wins in 24 games. He was a Heisman candidate in 1983 and the university mailed vinyl records of a song titled, "Ole Hoss, the Ballad of West Virginia's Jeff Hostetler," to sportswriters to promote his candidacy.

7. Jesse Palmer, who was the second Canadian national to start at quarterback in an NFL game, became the first professional athlete to appear on *The Bachelor* television show in 2004. He started three games in four seasons with the Giants and finished his career with three touchdown passes and four interceptions.

8. Scott Brunner was named the Giants' starting quarterback for the 1983 season but he became a journeyman quarterback in rapid fashion. An NCAA Division II Hall-of-Famer, Brunner was traded to the Denver Broncos,

Green Bay Packers and St. Louis Cardinals in the span of 16 months.

9. Although Craig Kupp failed to make the Giants' roster after being drafted in the fifth round of the 1990 NFL Draft, both his father and son enjoyed success in the league. His father Jake was a talented offensive lineman who was inducted into the New Orleans Saints Hall of Fame in 1991 and his son Cooper had a breakout season with the Los Angeles Rams in 2019 with 94 catches for 1,161 yards and 10 touchdowns.

10. Charlie Conerly was a fierce competitor who impressed his teammates with his high tolerance for pain. In the book, *Vince: A Personal Biography of Vince Lombardi* by Michael O'Brien, the legendary coach recalled how Conerly broke his nose in a game. Instead of coming out of the game, the quarterback called two consecutive timeouts so that the trainer could push his nose back into place so he could continue to play.

CHAPTER 4:

THE PASS CATCHERS

QUIZ TIME!

1. Which Giants receiver suffered a self-inflicted gunshot wound during the 2008 regular season?

    a. Steve Smith

    b. Sinorice Moss

    c. Mario Manningham

    d. Plaxico Burress

2. Wide receiver Amani Toomer is the nephew of actor and comedian George Wallace.

    a. True

    b. False

3. The Giants drafted LSU wide receiver Odell Beckham Jr. in the first round of the 2014 NFL Draft. Which award did he win after his rookie season?

    a. AP NFL Most Valuable Player

    b. AP Offensive Rookie of the Year

    c. AP NFC Offensive Player of the Year

    d. AP NFL Offensive Player of the Year

4. Wide receiver Homer Jones was one of Fran Tarkenton's favorite targets in 1968 and made the Pro Bowl. How many years passed until another Giants receiver would make the Pro Bowl?

   a. 28
   b. 33
   c. 38
   d. 42

5. From 1970 through 1977, the Giants featured one of the best tight ends in the NFL who collected 327 receptions and 22 touchdowns. What was his name?

   a. Al Dixon
   b. Bill Helms
   c. Larry Kohn
   d. Bob Tucker

6. Which New York wide receiver led the NFL with a kickoff return average of 26.9 yards in 2004 and was the first Giant to lead the league in average kickoff return yardage since Clarence Childs in 1964?

   a. Jamaar Taylor
   b. Willie Ponder
   c. David Tyree
   d. Kevin Walter

7. Odell Beckham became the first player to record more than 75 receptions, 1,100 yards and 10 touchdowns as a rookie.

a. True

b. False

8. Which former wide receiver was named the director of player development for the Giants in 2014?

   a. Odessa Turner

   b. Thomas Lewis

   c. David Tyree

   d. Joe Jurevicius

9. Ron Dixon scored the only points for the Giants in Super Bowl XXXV with a long kickoff return for a touchdown. He also returned another kickoff for a touchdown in the Divisional playoffs that same postseason from the exact distance. How many yards were his kickoff return touchdowns?

   a. 94

   b. 97

   c. 99

   d. 102

10. Which of the following receivers underwent posterior spine stabilization surgery during his rookie season after receiving a brutal hit from Jacksonville safety Chris Hudson?

    a. Mark Ingram

    b. Nate Singleton

    c. Stephen Baker

    d. Ike Hilliard

11. Wide receiver Victor Cruz set the franchise record for most receiving yards in a single season in 2011 with 1,536 yards. Which one of the following receivers previously held the record?

    a. Ramses Barden
    b. Ike Hilliard
    c. Amani Toomer
    d. Bobby Joe Conrad

12. Sterling Shepard's father, Derrick, was a speedy quarterback who led the Oklahoma Sooners to a national championship in 1985.

    a. True
    b. False

13. Former Giants receiver Mark Ingram and his son, Mark Jr., were both selected in the first round and made history as it was the first time a father and son were drafted with the same pick in the NFL Draft. Which pick were they both drafted?

    a. 28th
    b. 22nd
    c. 25th
    d. 19th

14. Which New York Giants receiver is credited as the first player to "spike" the football into the field after scoring a touchdown?

    a. Don Herrmann
    b. Rich Houston

c. Coleman Zeno

d. Homer Jones

15. In 1992, Giants wide receiver Stephen Baker had the worst catch rate of any wide receiver in the NFL from 1991–2011. What percentage of the passes thrown to him did he catch?

a. 57.4%

b. 52.6%

c. 28.8%

d. 41.3%

16. Which Giants tight end wrote a book, *Rough & Tumble*, which detailed the fictional life of an NFL player named Dominic Fucillo and the struggles he faced while playing professional football.

a. Howard Cross

b. Mark Bavaro

c. Bob Tucker

d. Jeremy Shockey

17. Emery Moorehead and his son Aaron were the NFL's first father and son to have both played in and won Super Bowls.

a. True

b. False

18. Which Giants receiver became the first non-quarterback with multiple passing touchdowns in a season since Antwaan Randle El achieved the feat in 2010?

a. Victor Cruz

b. Odessa Turner

c. Johnny Perkins

d. Odell Beckham

19. Giants 2009 third-round pick Ramses Barden was the tallest wide receiver in team history. How tall was the former Cal Poly standout?

a. 6-foot-4.5 inches

b. 6-foot-7.5 inches

c. 6-foot-6.5 inches

d. 6-foot-5.5 inches

20. Homer Jones averaged 22.3 yards per reception during his career, which is still an NFL record for players with at least 200 receptions.

a. True

b. False

QUIZ ANSWERS

1. D - Plaxico Burress

2. A - True

3. B - AP Offensive Rookie of the Year

4. C - 38 (David Tyree, 2005)

5. D - Bob Tucker

6. B - Willie Ponder

7. A - True

8. C - David Tyree

9. B - 97

10. D - Ike Hilliard

11. C - Amani Toomer

12. B - False

13. A - 28th

14. D - Homer Jones

15. C - 28.8%

16. B - Mark Bavaro

17. A - True

18. D - Odell Beckham

19. C - 6-foot-6.5 inches

20. A - True

DID YOU KNOW?

1. Although he was born in Anchorage, Alaska, Steve Smith attended high school in California and was a standout basketball player. One of his former teammates at Taft High School in the San Fernando Valley was former Los Angeles Lakers point guard Jordan Farmar.

2. Lionel Manuel, who won a pair of Super Bowls with the Giants, attended the Scottsdale Culinary Institute after his football career was over and became a professional chef and restaurateur.

3. Before being traded to the Cleveland Browns in 2019, Odell Beckham inked the biggest shoe contract in NFL history. Nike signed the talented wideout to a five-year, $25 million deal in 2017 that could be worth $48 million over eight years if all the incentives are met.

4. Former sixth-round draft pick David Tyree was a troubled youth who battled alcohol addiction as a teenager. With the help of his wife, he became a Super Bowl champion with the Giants and is a born-again Christian who has made several appearances at "Battle Cry" Christian concerts to spread the gospel of Jesus Christ.

5. Amani Toomer caught only 44 passes during his first three NFL seasons and attributed his lack of production to exercise-induced asthma, which he had kept secret for many years. But his career took off after receiving treatment

for his condition and he averaged 77 receptions over the next four seasons.

6. Ed McCaffrey won a pair of Super Bowl rings with the Giants and in 2019 was named the head football coach at the University of Northern Colorado. He also has had his own line of condiments, including horseradish sauce and several varieties of mustard, for more than two decades.

7. A first-round selection in 1987, Mark Ingram caught 136 passes and 11 touchdowns in six seasons with the Giants. Unfortunately, life after football was not too kind to Ingram and he spent several years in a low-security United States federal prison for money laundering and fraud. He was granted his release from prison in 2015.

8. To say that the Giants had a bad Week 5 during the 2017 regular season is a gross understatement. In a matchup against the Los Angeles Chargers, New York lost three wide receivers to season-ending injuries. Odell Beckham (fractured fibula), Brandon Marshall (ankle) and Dwayne Harris (fractured foot) all had surgery and missed the final 11 games of the season.

9. In 2008, Giants receiver Steve Smith was the victim of an armed robbery. The University of Southern California product had just arrived home in Clifton, New Jersey when he was approached from behind by a man who put a gun to his head and demanded everything he had. Smith calmly handed over his money, jewelry and cell phone and the gunman left without any further incident.

10. Former Giants tight end Mark Bavaro is a passionate anti-abortion activist who is guided by his Catholic faith. He was one of 503 non-violent protesters arrested in 1988 during an anti-abortion rally.

CHAPTER 5:

RUNNING WILD

QUIZ TIME!

1. Which future Hall of Fame running back did the Giants sign before the 1976 season to replace the retired Ron Johnson?

    a. Greg Pruitt

    b. Larry Csonka

    c. Mike Thomas

    d. Floyd Little

2. Halfback Gene "Choo-Choo" Roberts rushed for 218 yards on Nov. 12, 1950, setting a team record that would stand for over 50 years.

    a. True

    b. False

3. Which Giants rookie running back led the league in punt return yards in 1989 and earned a trip to the Pro Bowl?

    a. Jon Francis

    b. Dana Wright

c. Dave Meggett

d. Tim Richardson

4. David Wilson, a first-round pick in 2012, retired after only two seasons because of a career-ending injury. Which type of injury did he suffer?

a. Back

b. Knee

c. Ankle

d. Neck

5. Which pair of Giants running backs both rushed for over 1,000 yards in 2008 to help New York lead the NFL in rushing yards?

a. Brandon Jacobs and Derrick Ward

b. Ottis Anderson and Joe Morris

c. Joe Montgomery and Tiki Barber

d. Ahmad Bradshaw and Tyrone Wheatley

6. During the second week of the 2018 season, in a loss to the Dallas Cowboys, Saquon Barkley set a franchise record for catches in a game and tied the NFL single-game record for most receptions by a rookie in a single-game. How many catches did he have against the Cowboys?

a. 10

b. 12

c. 14

d. 17

7. Ahmad Bradshaw scored his first NFL touchdown on a 98-yard run in the fourth quarter against the Buffalo Bills in 2007.

   a. True
   b. False

8. Which one of the following running backs became the first Giant to gain 1,000 yards rushing in a season?

   a. Billy Taylor
   b. Alex Webster
   c. Bobby Duhon
   d. Ron Johnson

9. Tiki Barber holds the NFL record for most 200-yard rushing games by a player over 30 years old. How many times did he rush for over 200 yards after his 30th birthday?

   a. 2
   b. 3
   c. 4
   d. 5

10. Which Giants running back scored his first career touchdown in his NFL debut, which was also his 23rd birthday?

   a. Andre Brown
   b. Wayne Gallman
   c. Butch Woolfolk
   d. Rashad Jennings

11. Which one of the following running backs finished his sophomore campaign as the only running back in Giants' history to rush for 1,000 yards in each of his first two seasons?

    a. Tiki Barber
    b. Leon Perry
    c. Paul Perkins
    d. Saquon Barkley

12. Tiki Barber set a new team single-game rushing record with 220 yards and broke his own single-season record in a 2005 victory over the Kansas City Chiefs.

    a. True
    b. False

13. Butch Woolfolk set what was then the NFL record in 1983 for most rushing attempts in a single game. How many carries did he have in the Giants 23-0 victory over the Philadelphia Eagles?

    a. 40
    b. 41
    c. 43
    d. 47

14. Which Giants running back was called to testify before a 2003 federal grand jury investigating a laboratory that had produced performance-enhancing drugs for professional athletes?

    a. Joe Morris
    b. Tyrone Wheatley

c. Ottis Anderson

d. Butch Woolfolk

15. Which Giants running back was the franchise all-time scoring leader with 319 points before he was traded to the Chicago Cardinals in 1946?

a. Kelly Moan

b. Walt Nielsen

c. Mario Tonelli

d. Ward Cuff

16. Giants rookie Joe Morris scored a touchdown on his first NFL carry but he was initially known for his lack of height. How tall was the former Syracuse All-American?

a. 5-foot-5

b. 5-foot-6

c. 5-foot-7

d. 5-foot-8

17. New York Giants halfback Gene "Choo-Choo" Roberts led the NFL with 17 touchdowns in 1949.

a. True

b. False

18. Which former Giant became an actor and portrayed a young George Foreman in the Emmy-Award-winning HBO film, *Don King: Only in America*?

a. John Conner

b. Jarrod Bunch

c. Everson Walls

d. Carl Lockhart

19. Which former Giants running back made his Broadway debut in 2019 as Don in *Kinky Boots*?

    a. Gary Brown
    b. Paul Perkins
    c. Tiki Barber
    d. Rodney Hampton

20. The Giants' 1991 first-round pick Jarrod Bunch lost the fourth toe on his right foot at the age of five in a lawnmower accident.

    a. True
    b. False

QUIZ ANSWERS

1. B - Larry Csonka

2. A - True

3. C - Dave Meggett

4. D - Neck

5. A - Brandon Jacobs and Derrick Ward

6. C - 14

7. B - False

8. D - Ron Johnson

9. C - 4

10. B - Wayne Gallman

11. D - Saquon Barkley

12. A - True

13. C - 43

14. B - Tyrone Wheatley

15. D - Ward Cuff

16. C - 5-foot-7

17. A - True

18. B - Jarrod Bunch

19. C - Tiki Barber

20. A – True

DID YOU KNOW

1. Tuffy Leemans was the 18th player chosen in the 1936 NFL Draft, but he was the only rookie to be tabbed by the league as a 1936 First-Team All-Pro Team selection. The talented fullback averaged 69.2 rushing yards per game and led the NFL in rushing with 830 yards.

2. Hank Soar enjoyed a nine-year career with the Giants and was the hero of the 1938 NFL Championship Game after catching the title-clinching touchdown pass to defeat the Green Bay Packers. He also was a Major League Baseball umpire who was the first base umpire for two historic no-hitters by New York Yankees hurler Don Larsen and California Angels fireballer Nolan Ryan.

3. Frank Gifford was an eight-time Pro Bowler who was inducted into the Pro Football Hall of Fame in 1977. His wife, television personality Kathie Lee Gifford, said after his death in 2015 that he grew up in a poverty-stricken family that lived in almost 30 different places as a child due to his father seeking employment during the Depression. She also said that the Gifford and his family sometimes ate dog food to survive.

4. Although Tiki and Ronde Barber were not the first set of identical twins to play in the NFL, they are certainly the most famous pair of look-a-like brothers to lace up their cleats on any given Sunday. Tiki rushed for over 10,000

yards for the Giants and was invited to three Pro Bowls, while Ronde was named to the Pro Bowl team five times and remains the Tampa Bay Buccaneers' all-time leader in interceptions with 47.

5. Dave Meggett was an exciting punt and kickoff returner for the Giants who had eight touchdown returns during his career. But the 1989 fifth-round pick was plagued with legal and financial trouble after his football career ended. He escaped serious consequences numerous times for sexually or physically assaulting several women. But his luck ran out in 2010 when he was given a 30-year prison sentence for robbing and raping a College of Charleston student.

6. Brandon Jacobs, who found the end zone 60 times during his NFL career and won two Super Bowl rings with the Giants, appeared on the ABC television *Shark Tank* in 2012 to help pitch a protein supplement/energy drink with Pro NRG founder, Tania Patruno. The duo successfully bagged a $250,000 investment and the business initially had robust sales. But the business quickly foundered due to heavy competition and imitation products.

7. Former Giants running back Michael Cox's father was the subject of the book, *The Fence*, which was penned by former *Boston Globe* reporter Dick Lehr. The elder Cox was a police officer with the Boston Police Department who was severely beaten one night in 1995 while working in plain clothes by a group of his fellow officers.

8. Saquon Barkley was rewarded by his teammates for his outstanding play and work ethic during his rookie season by being selected as one of the seven team captains for the Giants during his sophomore campaign. This honor is rarely given to a player after only one year on the team.

9. Giants running back Paul Perkins was the third member of his family to carry the rock in the NFL. His father, Bruce, had short stints with the Tampa Bay Buccaneers and Indianapolis Colts, while his uncle, Don, was a member of the Dallas Cowboys for eight seasons.

10. Jarrod Bunch played three unproductive seasons with the Giants but has some impressive acting credits, including the role of the young George Foreman in the Emmy-Award-winning HBO film, *Don King: Only in America*.

CHAPTER 6:

IN THE TRENCHES

QUIZ TIME!

1. Which former Giants defensive tackle appeared on an episode of the television show *Love Boat* in 1979?

    a. Ron Nery

    b. Rosey Grier

    c. John Kompara

    d. Bob Watters

2. In 1938, Giants Hall-of-Famer Mel Hein became the only offensive lineman in the history of the NFL to win the league MVP award?

    a. True

    b. False

3. Offensive tackle Rosey Brown was a nine-time Pro Bowl selection who appeared in 162 games for the Giants over 13 seasons. How many games did he miss during his career in New York?

    a. 8

    b. 6

c. 4

d. 7

4. Which former Giants offensive lineman was the first former NFL player to share publicly that he was HIV-positive?

   a. Billy Ard
   b. Randy Pass
   c. Dan Fowler
   d. Roy Simmons

5. Art Donovan was a fixture on one television show and made 10 appearances to share funny stories about his playing days. What was the name of this television program?

   a. *Late Show with David Letterman*
   b. *Phil Donahue Show*
   c. *Tonight Show with Johnny Carson*
   d. *Ed Sullivan Show*

6. Which defensive tackle made one of the biggest plays in franchise history during the 1990 NFC Championship game when he forced San Francisco 49ers running back Roger Craig to fumble the football with less than three minutes remaining in the game?

   a. Jon Carter
   b. Brad Henke
   c. Otis Moore
   d. Erik Howard

7. A first-round draft pick in 1966, Francis Peay was the first African-American head coach in the Big Ten Conference when he was hired by Northwestern University in 1986.

   a. True
   b. False

8. Which former player was incredibly popular in the 1970s for his unusual hobbies of needlepoint and macramé?

   a. Dick Nolan
   b. Jimmy Patton
   c. Rosey Grier
   d. Mel Triplett

9. Which one of the following names did offensive tackle Will Beatty choose for his own clothing line?

   a. The William Beatty Apparel Company
   b. Will Beatty Collection
   c. WB Classic Brand
   d. Beatty Apparel Co.

10. Which Giants' first-round draft pick tested positive for the banned substance ostarine and was ruled ineligible for the 2019 College Football Playoff?

    a. Avery Moss
    b. Dexter Lawrence
    c. R.J. McIntosh
    d. Lorenzo Carter

11. Which former first-round draft pick signed a three-year, $30 million contract with the Miami Dolphins on March 20, 2020?

a. Markus Kuhn

b. Damontre Moore

c. Ereck Flowers

d. Justin Pugh

12. Hall of Fame center-linebacker Mel Hein never missed a game during his 15 seasons in the NFL.

a. True

b. False

13. Which Giants offensive lineman was the first player to be ejected for two unsportsmanlike conduct penalties in the same game in 2016 under a new rule that the NFL implemented at the beginning of the 2016 season?

a. Mitch Petrus

b. Will Beatty

c. James Brewer

d. Weston Richburg

14. Which Giants' first-round pick in 2013 was the highest-drafted offensive lineman selected from Syracuse since 1954?

a. Matt McCants

b. Justin Pugh

c. Bobby Hart

d. Brandon Mosley

15. The Giants signed offensive tackle Rosey Brown to a team-friendly contract in 1953 because he was a late-round draft pick. How much did Brown earn his rookie season?

a. $3,500

b. $4,000

c. $4,500

d. $5,000

16. Giants defensive tackle Marcus Kuhn did not start playing football until the age of 14 because he grew up in soccer-crazed Europe. He was also the first citizen of his country to score a touchdown in the NFL. Which country was he born in?

a. Austria

b. France

c. Germany

d. Sweden

17. Former Giants center Brian Williams has a son, Maxx, who is a tight end that was drafted in the first round by the Arizona Cardinals.

a. True

b. False

18. Which Giants offensive lineman received All-Madden honors in both 1990 and 1991?

a. Greg Bishop

b. Jumbo Elliott

c. Scott Davis

d. Bob Kratch

19. Which Giants Hall-of-Famer was banned from playing football in high school because his older brother was injured playing football and died?

a. Sam Huff

b. Mel Hein

c. Rosey Brown

d. Rosey Grier

20. In each of his first three seasons, defensive tackle Art Donovan played for a team that went out of business.

a. True

b. False

QUIZ ANSWERS

1. B - Rosey Grier

2. A - True

3. C - 4

4. D - Roy Simmons

5. A - *Late Show with David Letterman*

6. D - Erik Howard

7. B - False (2nd, Dennis Green)

8. C - Rosey Grier

9. A - The William Beatty Apparel Company

10. B - Dexter Lawrence

11. C - Ereck Flowers

12. B - False

13. D - Weston Richburg

14. B - Justin Pugh

15. A - $3,500

16. C - Germany

17. B - False

18. B - Jumbo Elliott

19. C - Rosey Brown

20. A – True

DID YOU KNOW?

1. Rosey Grier worked as a bodyguard for Senator Robert Kennedy during the 1968 presidential campaign. The former defensive tackle was guarding Ethel Kennedy when Sirhan Sirhan shot Senator Kennedy but rushed to the scene and subdued the gunman while taking the gun.

2. Art Donovan was the first professional football player to be selected for the U.S. Marine Corps Hall of Fame. The former Giant was a decorated war hero who received both the Asiatic-Pacific Campaign Medal and the Philippine Liberation Medal.

3. The Giants drafted tackle Art Lewis with the ninth overall pick in the 1936 NFL Draft but, after only one season in New York, he opted to coach at Ohio Wesleyan University. The following year he joined the Cleveland Rams as a player-coach and became the youngest head coach in NFL history at the age of 27 when he was named interim head coach in the middle of the season.

4. Rich Baldinger had two brothers who also played in the NFL. His older brother, Brian, played for the Dallas Cowboys, Indianapolis Colts and Philadelphia Eagles. His younger brother, Gary, was a teammate on the Kansas City Chiefs and also suited up for the Buffalo Bills and the Colts.

5. Rosey Brown was such a big kid when he was growing up

that he was promoted to the third grade at the age of six after he passed a test. Thus, because he skipped both the first and second grades, Brown was only 15 years old when he graduated high school. He was only 19 when he finished college and had yet to celebrate his 20th birthday when he played his first game with the Giants in 1953.

6. New York made history in 1996 by selected University of Louisville offensive tackle Roman Oben in the third round. He was the first Cameroon national to get drafted by an NFL team and he started 48 of 50 games during his four seasons with the Giants.

7. Boston College offensive lineman Chris Snee must have felt at home when the Giants drafted him in the second round of the 2004 NFL Draft. His father-in-law, Tom Coughlin, was the head coach of New York at that time.

8. Defensive lineman Jay Alford won championships in both the National Football League and the United Football League. He was a member of the Giants squad that upset the undefeated New England Patriots in Super Bowl XLII and in 2011 he was a key player that helped the Virginia Destroyers win the UFL championship in their inaugural season.

9. Former New York defensive tackle Linval Joseph was a member of the Minnesota Vikings in 2014 when he suffered a minor injury after a gunman shot nine people at a Minneapolis nightclub. Joseph started 46 of 53 regular-season games during his four years with the Giants but

blossomed into a two-time Pro Bowl player with the Vikings.

10. Former University of Miami defensive tackle William Joseph had an uninspiring NFL career despite being picked in the first round by the Giants in 2003. He was sentenced to two years in prison in 2012 for his involvement in an alleged scheme to steal people's identities and file fraudulent tax returns.

CHAPTER 7:

THE BACK SEVEN

QUIZ TIME!

1. In which year did Lawrence Taylor win both the NFL's Defensive Rookie of the Year and Defensive Player of the Year awards?

   a. 1979
   b. 1980
   c. 1981
   d. 1982

2. Linebacker Corey Miller played eight seasons with the Giants and his son, Christian, was drafted in the fourth round by the Carolina Panthers in 2019.

   a. True
   b. False

3. Which defensive back was disciplined for posting on Twitter during a game against the Dallas Cowboys?

   a. Aaron Ross
   b. Eli Apple

c. Janoris Jenkins

d. Prince Amukamara

4. Which Giants long snapper was a two-time Pro Bowl selection?

a. Jay Alford

b. Danny Aiken

c. Trey Junkin

d. Zak DeOssie

5. Which controversial issue led former Giant Myron Guyton and a trio of former players to file a lawsuit against the NFL in 2012?

a. Steroids

b. Insurance

c. Concussions

d. Pain pills

6. Which Giants player won the ABC television *Superstars* competition three consecutive years during the NFL offseason?

a. Jason Sehorn

b. Mark Collins

c. Phillippi Sparks

d. Terrell Thomas

7. Lawrence Taylor was suspended for the first four games of the 1988 season for his second violation of the league's substance-abuse policy.

a. True

b. False

8. Which former Giants linebacker suffered a severe back injury in 2007 while paragliding in Chile?

a. Dan Lloyd

b. Corey Widmer

c. Nick Greisen

d. Chase Blackburn

9. What type of injury diminished linebacker Jessie Armstead's draft stock, which led to him falling into the eighth round of the 1993 NFL Draft?

a. Back

b. Neck

c. Hamstring

d. Torn ACL

10. Which former Giants linebacker served as the New York Jets director of player development?

a. Gary Reasons

b. Brian Kelley

c. Carl Banks

d. Brad Van Pelt

11. Which former Giants cornerback became the Detroit Lions' interim general manager in 2015?

a. Mark Haynes

b. Sheldon White

c. Will Peterson

d. Perry Williams

12. Emlen Tunnell received the Silver Lifesaving Medal for heroism in rescuing a shipmate from flames during a torpedo attack in 1944 and two years later he rescued another shipmate who fell into the sea.

a. True
b. False

13. The Giants' 2004 first-round draft pick, Gibril Wilson, signed a free-agent contract with the Oakland Raiders in 2008 that made him one of the highest-paid safeties in NFL history. How much was his contract worth?

a. $39 million
b. $35 million
c. $42 million
d. $44 million

14. Which Giants assistant coach convinced future Hall of Fame linebacker Sam Huff to not quit football in 1956 after the rookie left camp because he was discouraged?

a. Tom Landry
b. Don Shula
c. Vince Lombardi
d. Don Coryell

15. Which hobby did former Giants linebacker Ryan Phillips enjoy the most before he was drafted in 1997?

a. Scuba diving
b. Pro wrestling
c. Bull rider
d. Skydiving

16. Which former All-Pro defensive back became a player-coach with the Giants before taking over an expansion team and becoming a Hall of Fame head coach?

    a. Hank Stram
    b. Tom Landry
    c. Sam Wyche
    d. George Allen

17. Linebacker Pepper Johnson wrote a book, *Win for All*, which detailed the Giants 1990 championship season.

    a. True
    b. False

18. Despite missing the first four games of the 1988 regular season, Lawrence Taylor still managed to register an insane number of sacks. What was his sack total that season?

    a. 10.5
    b. 12.5
    c. 15.5
    d. 17.5

19. Which of the following players became the first rookie middle linebacker to start an NFL championship game?

    a. Sam Huff
    b. Byron Hunt
    c. Harry Carson
    d. Lawrence Taylor

20. Giants long snapper Zak DeOssie's father, Steve, is a former NFL linebacker and the pair were the first father-son duo to win Super Bowls with the same franchise.

a. True
b. False

QUIZ ANSWERS

1. C - 1981

2. A - True

3. B - Eli Apple

4. D - Zak DeOssie

5. C - Concussions

6. A - Jason Sehorn

7. A - True

8. B - Corey Widmer

9. D - Torn ACL

10. C - Carl Banks

11. B - Sheldon White

12. A - True

13. A - $39 million

14. C - Vince Lombardi

15. D - Skydiving

16. B - Tom Landry

17. B - False

18. C - 15.5

19. A - Sam Huff

20. A – True

DID YOU KNOW?

1. The Giants broke the color barrier in 1948 by signing defensive back Emlen Tunnell as the first African-American player in franchise history. A six-time First-Team All-Pro selection, Tunnell was also the first African-American inducted into the Pro Football Hall of Fame.

2. Former Giants cornerback Dominique Rodgers-Cromartie has a pair of cousins who also were defensive backs in the NFL. Antonio Cromartie led the league with 10 interceptions in 2007 and was selected to four Pro Bowls, while Marcus Cromartie played briefly with the San Francisco 49ers and the Houston Texans. He is also a cousin of Indianapolis Colts cornerback Isaiah Rodgers.

3. Prince Amukamara's mother, Christy, is a former world-class sprinter who competed at the 1984 Summer Olympics for Nigeria in track and field. Amukamara won a Super Bowl ring during his five-year stint with the Giants.

4. Linebacker Greg Jones celebrated the Giants' victory in Super Bowl XLVI by proposing to his girlfriend on the field. A former Michigan State women's basketball player, Mandy Piechowski and Jones tied the knot in the summer of 2013.

5. The New York Giants' 2006 fifth-round draft pick Charlie Peprah's grandfather was the former military president of

Ghana. General Ignatius Kutu Acheampong ruled the African nation for more than six years but was executed by a firing squad after he was deposed in a palace coup.

6. Linebacker Harry Carson was the lucky charm for Giants' head coach Bill Parcells. During his time in New York, Parcells would have Carson stand beside him while the National Anthem played for good luck.

7. Cornerback Phillippi Sparks' daughter, Jordin, won the 2007 edition of *American Idol* and is a Grammy-nominated singer. Sparks played eight seasons with the Giants and was a member of a talented defensive backfield that included cornerback Jason Sehorn.

8. Aaron Ross met his future wife, Sanya Richards, at the University of Texas, where he played football and she was a track and field star. Richards is a four-time Olympic gold medalist and their wedding was showcased on the American reality television series *Platinum Weddings*. The couple's marriage was also featured on a weekly docuseries called *Sanya's Glam and Gold* on We TV.

9. Before chronic traumatic encephalopathy (CTE) and the long-term effects of concussions became a national topic, former Giants linebacker Harry Carson documented his struggles with post-concussion syndrome in his book, *Captain for Life*, in 2011. He was one of the first former NFL players to chronicle his personal experiences with concussions and CTE.

10. Jason Sehorn surprised his girlfriend, actress Angie

Harmon, with a marriage proposal that was witnessed on national television. With the help of talk show host Jay Leno, Sehorn hid backstage while Harmon was a guest on *The Tonight Show*. He suddenly appeared on the set and got on one knee to propose to Harmon in front of a studio audience and a national television audience.

CHAPTER 8:

ODDS & ENDS & AWARDS

QUIZ TIME!

1. Which Giants player is the only rookie to ever win the NFL Defensive Player of the Year award?

   a. Rosey Grier
   b. Sam Huff
   c. Lawrence Taylor
   d. Carl Lockhart

2. The Giants were known as a "team of nomads" in the 1970s and called four different stadiums their home - Yankee Stadium, the Yale Bowl, Shea Stadium and Giants Stadium.

   a. True
   b. False

3. The Giants tied the NFL record for most sacks in a game against the Philadelphia Eagles in 200 7. How many times did New York sack quarterback Donovan McNabb?

   a. 10
   b. 12

c. 13

d. 14

4. How many sacks did Giants defensive end Osi Umenyiora register in a 2007 game to set a new franchise record?

a. 3

b. 4

c. 5

d. 6

5. Which of the following players set the NFL single-season record for sacks in 2001?

a. Cedric Jones

b. Justin Tuck

c. Michael Strahan

d. Cornelius Griffin

6. Andy Robustelli was a three-time Pro Bowl selection who was also an iron man who rarely missed a game during his 14 years in the NFL. How many games did he miss during his career?

a. 1

b. 2

c. 3

d. 4

7. Linebacker Brandon Short earned his MBA in 2010 from Columbia Business School and began working for Goldman Sachs that same year.

a. True

b. False

8. In which year did Lawrence Taylor set the then-team record with 20.5 sacks?

   a. 1985
   b. 1986
   c. 1987
   d. 1988

9. Which former Giants defensive end played 13 seasons in the NFL and finished his career with 52 sacks after being drafted with the fifth overall pick in 1977?

   a. Erick Howard
   b. Leonard Marshall
   c. George Martin
   d. Gary Jeter

10. Which one of the following players played for the Giants for 10 seasons and was a two-time recipient of the NFL Defensive Lineman of the Year award?

    a. George Martin
    b. Erik Howard
    c. Leonard Marshall
    d. John Washington

11. Which five-time Pro Bowl defensive back was killed in an automobile accident in 1972?

    a. Jimmy Patton
    b. All Brenner
    c. Richard Perrin
    d. Jim Holifield

12. The Giants Osi Umenyiora is the only British citizen to ever win a Super Bowl ring.

   a. True
   b. False

13. Which Giants safety was named to the Pro Bowl in 1966 despite the Giants having one of the worst defensive teams in NFL history that allowed 38.5 points a game to opposing teams?

   a. Phil Harris
   b. Henry Carr
   c. Willie Williams
   d. Carl "Spider" Lockhart

14. Defensive end Oshane Ximines was taken by the Giants in the third round of the 2019 NFL Draft to become the first player from his college ever to get drafted. Which school did he attend?

   a. Cornell
   b. Old Dominion
   c. Davidson
   d. Harvard

15. Which Giants pass rusher had one of his fingers amputated in 2015 after he injured his hand in a fireworks accident?

   a. Devon Kennard
   b. Justin Tuck
   c. Jason Pierre-Paul
   d. Michael Strahan

16. How many combined sacks did Leonard Marshall and Lawrence Taylor have during the 1985 season?

    a. 28.5
    b. 25.5
    c. 30.5
    d. 32.5

17. Defensive end Fred Dryer, who played for the Giants for three seasons, is the only NFL player to score two safeties in the same game.

    a. True
    b. False

18. Which Giants cornerback was injured in a shooting accident less than one week after being drafted in the sixth round of the 2019 NFL Draft?

    a. Deandre Baker
    b. Julian Love
    c. Corey Ballentine
    d. Ryan Connelly

19. Which Giants linebacker founded his own limousine company after he retired and was also a former president of the National Limousine Association?

    a. Jeff Smith
    b. Ken Avery
    c. Henry Davis
    d. Ray Hickl

20. Lawrence Taylor is the only player in NFL history to win four Defensive Player of the Year Awards.

  a. True
  b. False

QUIZ ANSWERS

1. C - Lawrence Taylor

2. A - True

3. B - 12

4. D - 6

5. C - Michael Strahan

6. A - 1

7. A - True

8. B - 1986

9. D - Gary Jeter

10. C - Leonard Marshall

11. A - Jimmy Patton

12. B - False

13. D - Carl "Spider" Lockhart

14. B - Old Dominion

15. C - Jason Pierre-Paul

16. A - 28.5

17. A - True

18. C - Corey Ballentine

19. B - Ken Avery

20. B – False

DID YOU KNOW?

1. Although the New York Giants were receiving a hefty share of the proceeds from the NFL's television contract with CBS, the team owners strongly believed that the league would be stronger if the television revenue were shared equally among all franchises. The Giants, who were receiving $175,000 a game in the early 1960s due to its prime market area, made a financial sacrifice that allowed the NFL to grow into the most profitable professional sports league in the United States.

2. Hank Soar had a passion for baseball as well as football. He played semi-pro baseball and, during World War II, Philadelphia Athletics manager Connie Mack discovered him umpiring a baseball game while Soar was serving in the Army. He later served as crew chief for the famous 1969 World Series featuring the "Miracle Mets" and umpired in five World Series.

3. Andy Robustelli was a six-time First-Team All-Pro selection who also worked in the Giants' front office for six years. He was the only player who was on the field during the first two NFL games that were broadcast to a national audience.

4. Cornerback Terrell Thomas was the Giants' second-round pick in the 2008 NFL Draft and played in 12 games, including two starts, during his rookie season. However,

injuries derailed his promising career and he missed the entire season in both 2011 and 2012. He made an amazing comeback in 2013 to become only the second player in NFL history to play in the league again after suffering three torn ACLs in the same knee.

5. Corey Webster won a BCS National Championship with LSU and two Super Bowl rings with the Giants. But one of his most memorable moments as a player came in the 2007 NFC Championship game when he intercepted future Hall-of-Famer Brett Favre's last pass as a Green Bay Packer to set up the win and book the Giants a ticket to Super Bowl XLII.

6. Linebacker Brandon Short and rookie tight end Jeremy Shockey got into a fistfight during the 2002 training camp. The brawl started when Shockey refused to sing his college alma mater fight song in the cafeteria, which is a tradition for Giants rookies.

7. Fred Dryer was a talented defensive end who forced his way out of both New York and New England before finding a suitable home with the Los Angeles Rams. His career blossomed on and off the field on the West Coast and he enjoyed a successful career as an actor including his own television series, *Hunter*.

8. Although the New York Giants drafted Buck Buchanan in the 19th round of the 1963 NFL Draft, the AFL's Kansas City Chief made the future Hall of Fame defensive tackle the first African-American number one draft choice in the

history of professional football. He played in six AFL All-Star games and was a fixture on the Chiefs' defensive front for 166 consecutive games at one time during his 13-year career.

9. Defensive end Mathias Kiwanuka's grandfather was Benedicto Kiwanuka, who became Uganda's first prime minister after the country gained independence from British rule in 1961. He was executed by Idi Amin's murderous regime in 1972.

10. Leonard Marshall registered 83.5 sacks during his illustrious career but will always be remembered for the vicious hit that knocked San Francisco 49ers quarterback Joe Montana out of the 1991 NFC championship game. Marshall delivered a bone-crushing shot to the future Hall-of-Famer during the fourth quarter that resulted in a broken hand, cracked ribs and a bruised sternum and stomach. Montana exited the game and did not play another regular-season game for nearly two years.

CHAPTER 9:

NICKNAMES

QUIZ TIME!

1. Which former Giants Hall of Fame player was sometimes known as "Old Indestructible"?

    a. Y.A. Tittle

    b. Mel Hein

    c. Rosey Brown

    d. Frank Gifford

2. Brandon Jacobs was the "Earth" in the running back corps of the Giants nicknamed "Earth, Wind, & Fire" with Derrick Ward (Wind) and Ahmad Bradshaw (Fire).

    a. True

    b. False

3. What was the nickname of Giants quarterback Jeff Hostetler?

    a. Hossie

    b. The Host

    c. J-Boy

    d. Hoss

4. Which wide receiver played his entire career with the Giants and caught a touchdown pass in Super Bowl XXV to earn the nickname "The Touchdown Maker"?

   a. Victor Cruz

   b. Amani Toomer

   c. Stephen Baker

   d. Ike Hilliard

5. Which former New York running back was known as the "Great Dayne" in college?

   a. Alex Webster

   b. Joe Morris

   c. Ron Dayne

   d. Doug Kotar

6. Keith Hamilton was a ferocious pass rusher who played 12 seasons with the Giants and finished his career with 63 sacks. Which nickname was he given in the NFL?

   a. Hammer

   b. Chief

   c. Dr. Sack

   d. Thumper

7. Defensive end Justin Tuck was called "The Destroyer" by his Giants teammates.

   a. True

   b. False

8. What nickname did Joe Morrison's teammates call him because he played both wide receiver and running back at a consistently high level for the Giants?

a. Old Joe

b. Mr. Dependable

c. Mr. Reliable

d. Old Dependable

9. Which Hall of Fame defensive back was sometimes known as "The Gremlin"?

a. Jim Thorpe

b. Emlen Tunnell

c. Ray Flaherty

d. Tom Landry

10. Because of his impressive size and knack for breaking tackles, which Giants running back was known as the "Juggernaut"?

a. Ron Dayne

b. Ahmad Bradshaw

c. Brandon Jacobs

d. Ottis Anderson

11. Jason Pierre-Paul was known as the "Haitian Sensation" in college but was given a new nickname with the Giants. Which nickname was he given in the NFL?

a. JPP

b. J-Pop

c. Dr. Chaos

d. Mr. Sack

12. Carl Lockhart was a speedy defensive back who was nicknamed "Spider" by Giants assistant coach Emlen Tunnell.

a. True

b. False

13. New York boasted one of the league's top defensive units from 1986 to 1990. Which nickname was this group given?

a. Big Blue Crew

b. Legion of Doom

c. The Chain Gang

d. Big Blue Wrecking Crew

14. Which Giants quarterback is known as "Danny Dimes" for his ability to throw a football with precision accuracy?

a. Phil Simms

b. Daniel Jones

c. Kerry Collins

d. Eli Manning

15. Which nickname was given to a group of Giants linebackers that included Lawrence Taylor, Brad Van Pelt, Harry Carson and Brian Kelley?

a. Crunch Bunch

b. The G Force

c. Masters of Pain

d. Men of Pain

16. What nickname did ESPN sportscaster Chris Berman begin calling the New York Giants in the mid-1980s?

a. Jints

b. G-Team

c. G-Men

d. Blue Men

17. New York Giants players referred to team owner Wellington Mara as "The Duke" because he was named after the Duke of Wellington.

    a. True
    b. False

18. Which nickname did former Giants head coach Bill Parcells attain when he was an assistant with the New England Patriots?

    a. Tiger
    b. Tuna
    c. Snake
    d. Shark

19. Which nickname did Janoris Jenkins' coach give him in college because he did not know the defensive plays and was moving around everywhere fast?

    a. Flash
    b. Wheels
    c. Speedy
    d. Jackrabbit

20. Giants Land is the nickname used for both the New York Giants organization and the fan base of the team.

    a. True
    b. False

QUIZ ANSWERS

1. B - Mel Hein

2. A - True

3. D - Hoss

4. C - Stephen Baker

5. C - Ron Dayne

6. A - Hammer

7. B - False

8. D - Old Dependable

9. B - Emlen Tunnell

10. C - Brandon Jacobs

11. A - JPP

12. A -True

13. D - Big Blue Wrecking Crew

14. B - Daniel Jones

15. A - Crunch Bunch

16. C - G-Men

17. A - True

18. B - Tuna

19. D - Jackrabbit

20. B – False

DID YOU KNOW?

1. Running back John Fuqua, who played only one season for the Giants, was one of the NFL's sharpest dressers who gave himself the nicknamed "The French Count." He sometimes wore platform shoes that had transparent heels containing water and a live tropical fish from his own aquarium to match the color of his outfit.

2. Jared Lorenzen was a burly southpaw quarterback who was nicknamed "Pillsbury Throwboy" by his teammates since he weighed nearly 300 pounds during his short NFL career. His weight ballooned to 500 pounds in 2017 but he lost over 100 pounds before his untimely death in 2019 at the age of 38.

3. Former Giants wide receiver Odell Beckham was so impressed by the size of rookie running Saquon Barkley's legs during training camp in 2018 that he quickly nicknamed him "SaQuads." Barkley became the 2018 Pepsi NFL Rookie of the Year and Offensive Rookie of the Year after his maiden season in professional football.

4. Pete Henry was a 5-foot-11, 250-pound lineman who was called "Fats" because he did not have a weight-lifting or sculptured look. He played only four games for the Giants and served as the head coach of the Pottsville Maroons in 1928.

5. Hall-of-Famer Alphonse Emil Leemans was known as

"Tuffy" because of his playing style. "He was called Tuffy because he was tough," noted teammate Mel Hein. He led the NFL in rushing as a rookie and was selected as a First-Team All-Pro twice during his eight seasons with the Giants.

6. Nose tackle Damon Harrison was a big man who stood 6-foot-3 and weighed 350 pounds. He played three seasons with the Giants. Former Jets defensive line coach Karl Dunbar nicknamed him "Snacks" because he was always snacking in the meeting rooms.

7. The "Manning Bowl" referred to the three NFL games that pitted brothers Peyton and Eli Manning against each other. Older brother Peyton dominated his little brother Eli by posting a perfect 3-0 record in those head-to-head matchups.

8. Giants defensive Emlen Tunnell was an exceptional athlete who intercepted 79 passes for 1,282 yards during his NFL career, including four touchdowns. He was also a dynamic kick and punt return specialist who tallied 3,424 return yards and six touchdowns. He was called the Giants' "offense on defense" because he resembled a running back whenever he intercepted a pass.

9. Eli Manning was nicknamed "ELIte" by Giants fans after the signal-caller claimed in a preseason interview that he considered himself an elite quarterback in the same class as New England Patriots star Tom Brady. Manning cemented his claim as an elite quarterback by guiding the

Giants to a pair of Super Bowl victories over Brady and the Patriots.

10. Thomas "Pepper" Johnson won two Super Bowls as a player with the Giants and three Super Bowl rings as a coach with the New England Patriots. His aunt gave him the nickname "Pepper" because he had an unusual habit of putting black pepper on his corn flakes.

CHAPTER 10:

ALMA MATERS

QUIZ TIME!

1. Which former Giants wide receiver set a record while playing in for the University of Connecticut with 36 straight games with a catch, and finished his collegiate career with 165 receptions?

   a. Steve Smith

   b. Earnest Gray

   c. Geremy Davis

   d. Lionel Manuel

2. Davis Webb was the first quarterback in Texas Tech history to pass for over 400 yards twice in his freshman season.

   a. True

   b. False

3. Which former Giants quarterback was the leading rusher and passer for the Cornell University Big Red every year in which he was the starter?

a. Earl Morrall

b. Gary Wood

c. Benny Friedman

d. Fran Tarkenton

4. Rueben Randle was a five-star recruit and the top wide receiver prospect in the nation coming out of high school. Which school did he sign with on National Signing Day?

a. SMU

b. TCU

c. LSU

d. BYU

5. Which future Giants receiver set a then Orange Bowl record with three touchdown catches in 2005 to help USC trounce Oklahoma in the national championship game?

a. Rueben Randle

b. Johnny Perkins

c. Bobby Johnson

d. Steve Smith

6. Thomas Lewis caught a 99-yard touchdown pass in 1993 to equal the NCAA record for the longest touchdown pass in Division I football history. He also set two Big Ten records, including the most receiving yards (285) in a single game. Which Big Ten college did Lewis play for?

a. Indiana University

b. University of Iowa

c. University of Maryland

d. University of Minnesota

7. UCLA running back Paul Perkins led the Pac-12 in rushing in 2014 with 1,575 yards.

    a. True
    b. False

8. Ron Dayne was a 1999 consensus All-American who joined an elite company of eight running backs who rushed for over 1,000 in each of their four collegiate seasons. Which college did he attend?

    a. University of Notre Dame
    b. Boise State University
    c. University of Wisconsin
    d. Penn State University

9. Which New York running back played collegiate football for the Evansville Purple Aces, Illinois Fighting Illini and Northwestern Wildcats?

    a. Rashad Jennings
    b. Sean Bennett
    c. Brandon Jacobs
    d. Joe Morrison

10. Tyrone Wheatley was a two-sport standout at Michigan who was a Big Ten champion in which track and field event?

    a. Triple jump
    b. Pole vault
    c. Shot put
    d. 110-meter hurdles

11. Giants fullback Ward Cuff set a school record in the javelin throw and was the heavyweight boxing champion at which college?

    a. Marquette
    b. Michigan
    c. Auburn
    d. Texas A&M

12. Butch Woolfolk was an All-American sprinter at the University of Michigan and the Big Ten champion in two track and field events.

    a. True
    b. False

13. Which of the Giants' top overall draft picks won the best blocker award in the Southeastern Conference in 1963 and 1964 while playing football at Auburn University?

    a. Francis Peay
    b. Lou Cordileone
    c. Joe Don Looney
    d. Tucker Frederickson

14. Offensive tackle Scott Gragg was credited with 82 knockdown blocks during his senior season at which school?

    a. University of Maine
    b. University of Montana
    c. University of Washington
    d. University of Oregon

15. Dominique Rodgers-Cromartie was a versatile athlete who played cornerback, wide receiver and kickoff returner for which HBCU school?

    a. Tuskegee University
    b. Hampton University
    c. Tennessee State University
    d. Grambling University

16. Which University of Miami defensive tackle started all 51 games in his college career before playing five seasons with the Giants?

    a. William Joseph
    b. Leonard Marshall
    c. Justin Tuck
    d. George Martin

17. Cooper Taylor was diagnosed with Parkinson's disease while playing football at Georgia Tech but made a full recovery and played three seasons with the Giants.

    a. True
    b. False

18. Clint Sintim was a dominant college player who led the NCAA in sacks by a linebacker during his senior year for which school?

    a. University of Wisconsin
    b. Michigan State University
    c. Texas Christian University
    d. University of Virginia

19. Which prestigious award did cornerback Aaron Ross win as a senior at the University of Texas for being the top defensive back in the country?

a. Jim Thorpe Award
b. Doak Walker Award
c. Sam Huff Award
d. Heisman Trophy

20. Darian Thompson broke Eric Weddle's record of 18 career interceptions in 2015 to become the all-time interception leader for the Mountain West Conference.

a. True
b. False

QUIZ ANSWERS

1. C - Geremy Davis

2. A - True

3. B - Gary Wood

4. C - LSU

5. D - Steve Smith

6. A - Indiana University

7. A - True

8. C - University of Wisconsin

9. B - Sean Bennett

10. D - 110-meter hurdles

11. A - Marquette

12. A - True

13. D - Tucker Frederickson

14. B - University of Montana

15. C - Tennessee State University

16. A - William Joseph

17. B - False

18. D - University of Virginia

19. A - Jim Thorpe Award

20. A - True

DID YOU KNOW?

1. Mel Hein was an all-around athlete at Washington State College (now Washington State University) and was named to the 1930 College Football All-America Team. He also competed on the school's track team for one season and played three seasons on the men's basketball team.

2. Hakeem Nicks was a record-setting wide receiver at the University of North Carolina, but the school placed an asterisk by his record four years after he left for the NFL due to academic fraud. Nicks also broke NCAA rules as one of five former players who provided cash and jewelry to Tar Heels players who had eligibility remaining in 2009 and 2010.

3. Danny Kanell was under center for Florida State in 1995 when the Virginia Cavaliers snapped the Seminoles' 29-game winning streak against ACC teams since joining the conference in 1992. Besides dashing the national championship hopes of Florida State, the Cavaliers also halted the third-longest conference winning streak in major-college football history.

4. Pat Brady, who played both quarterback and punter at the University of Nevada, established a record that cannot be broken in a 1950 game against Loyola Marymount. He booted a 99-yard punt, which is the longest possible under NCAA rules.

5. Fred Benners picked an opportune time to deliver a historic performance in a rare televised college football game that was broadcast to a national audience. He threw for 326 yards and four touchdowns to lead SMU to a 27-20 win over Notre Dame.

6. Sinorice Moss was a speedster who starred in track and field at the University of Miami. A world-class sprinter, he recorded personal bests of 6.42 seconds in the 55 meters and 10.50 seconds in the 100 meters during his college career.

7. Jamie Williams was a two-sport prep standout who wanted to play both basketball and football in college. He chose to attend the University of Nebraska because it was the only school that offered him scholarships for both sports.

8. Ahmad Bradshaw rushed for nearly 3,000 yards and 31 touchdowns during his college career at Marshall, but the Thundering Herd was not his first choice. He signed with the University of Virginia but never suited up for the Cavaliers because he was kicked off the team after getting arrested for underage drinking and running from the police.

9. Wide receiver Mario Manningham's professional career got off to a rocky start due to his fondness for marijuana and other issues. His draft stock plunged after it was reported he failed several drug tests while playing at the University of Michigan and he performed poorly on the

Wonderlic exam. He was still drafted in the third round and won a Super Bowl ring with the Giants.

10. David Wilson was a standout performer in both football and track and field at Virginia Tech. He competed in the long jump, triple jump and the 60-meter dash for the Hokies and placed sixth in the triple jump at the 2011 NCAA Championships to earn All-America honors. On the gridiron, he rushed for a school record 1,709 yards in his senior season and was named the 2011 ACC Offensive Player of the Year.

CHAPTER 11:

IN THE DRAFT ROOM

QUIZ TIME!

1. How many of the Giants' first-round picks have been inducted into the Pro Football Hall of Fame?

   a. 1
   b. 2
   c. 3
   d. 5

2. New York has drafted five players from the University of Notre Dame in the first round, the most from any college.

   a. True
   b. False

3. Which player has the distinction of being the first draft pick in the history of the New York Giants franchise?

   a. Ed Widseth
   b. Art Lewis
   c. Walt Nielsen
   d. Merle Hapes

4. The Giants have drafted 79 players in the first round as of 2020. How many of their opening-round picks have been used to draft a running back?

   a. 35
   b. 22
   c. 30
   d. 27

5. New York has held the first overall pick twice in the NFL Draft twice, in 1951 and 1965. Which players did the Giants select with the top pick?

   a. Kyle Rote and Tucker Frederickson
   b. Skip Minisi and Paul Page
   c. Frank Gifford and Travis Tidwell
   d. Rocky Thompson and Eldridge Small

6. The Giants have traded away their first-round pick on numerous occasions. How many years have there been when the Giants did not draft a player in the first round?

   a. 15
   b. 13
   c. 11
   d. 17

7. New York drafted Oklahoma linebacker Jimmy Files with the 13th overall pick in the 1970 NFL Draft. He once played an entire game with the name Flies on the back of his jersey due to a mistake by the equipment manager.

   a. True
   b. False

8. The Giants had the No. 1 pick in the 1965 NFL Draft and passed on Dick Butkus, Gale Sayers and Joe Namath to draft which player?

    a. John Hicks
    b. Lee Grosscup
    c. Jerry Hillebrand
    d. Tucker Frederickson

9. Which small-time school did nose tackle John Mendenhall attend before New York drafted him in the third round in 1972?

    a. Akron
    b. Grambling
    c. Arkansas State
    d. Stephen F. Austin

10. Despite not having a first-round pick in 1973, New York drafted a pair of linebackers who would become key members of one of the NFL's best group of linebackers. Which two members of the "Crunch Bunch" did the Giants draft that year?

    a. Dan Lloyd and Michael Brooks
    b. Bill Svoboda and Jim Files
    c. Brad Van Pelt and Brian Kelley
    d. Harry Carson and Gary Reasons

11. Which Ohio State offensive lineman did the Giants draft with the third overall pick in the 1974 NFL Draft?

    a. John Hicks
    b. John Hill

c. Tom Mullen

d. Jumbo Elliott

12. The Giants' top two picks in the 1972 NFL Draft, defensive back Eldridge Small and defensive tackle Larry Jacobson, were both out of the league in three years.

a. True

b. False

13. The Giants uncovered a gem in the 1965 NFL Draft when they took North Texas State defensive back Carl "Spider" Lockhart. In which round did New York draft the two-time Pro Bowl safety?

a. 10th

b. 13th

c. 15th

d. 21st

14. Which Giants linebacker was inducted into the Pro Football Hall of Fame 30 years after New York selected him with the 105th pick in the 1976 NFL Draft?

a. Brad Van Pelt

b. Lawrence Taylor

c. Sam Huff

d. Harry Carson

15. The Giants drafted Hall of Fame defensive end Michael Strahan in the second round of the 1993 NFL Draft. How many players were drafted before New York chose the Texas Southern product?

a. 39

b. 44

c. 47

d. 52

16. Which University Georgia tackle did the Giants take in the 2020 NFL Draft with the fourth overall selection?

    a. Matt Peart

    b. Ereck Flowers

    c. Andrew Thomas

    d. Will Hernandez

17. New York used the second overall pick in the 1948 NFL Draft to select University of Pennsylvania halfback-defensive back Skip Minisi. However, he retired after one season to study law and become an attorney.

    a. True

    b. False

18. Which quarterback did New York select in the first round of the 1992 supplemental draft that resulted in the Giants forfeiting their first-round pick in 1993?

    a. Kent Graham

    b. Dave Brown

    c. Kerry Collins

    d. Jeff Hostetler

19. Which All-American tight end did the Giants select in the second round of the 1981 NFL Draft (he caught only five passes for 49 yards during his lone season in New York)?

a. Steve Alvers

b. Malcolm Scott

c. Jamie Williams

d. Dave Young

20. New York has drafted three players with the fourth overall pick in the history of the franchise, but only one of those premium draft selections has played more than one season with the Giants.

a. True

b. False

QUIZ ANSWERS

1. C - 3

2. A - True

3. B - Art Lewis

4. D - 27

5. A - Kyle Rote and Tucker Frederickson

6. C - 11

7. A - True

8. D - Tucker Frederickson

9. B - Grambling

10. C - Brad Van Pelt and Brian Kelley

11. A - John Hicks

12. A - True

13. B - 13th

14. D - Harry Carson

15. A - 39

16. C - Andrew Thomas

17. A - True

18. B - Dave Brown

19. D - Dave Young

20. A – True

DID YOU KNOW?

1. Fullback Joe Don Looney lasted only 28 days with the Giants after being selected with the 12th overall pick in the 1964 NFL Draft. He was a moody character who was traded three times during his first three years in the league. He once argued with a couple about politics and later that same evening broke into their apartment and attacked them.

2. In 1967, the NFL and the AFL held a "common draft" for the first time. Because of their trade with the Minnesota Vikings to acquire quarterback Fran Tarkenton, the Giants did not have a pick in the first three rounds. Thus, the team missed out in a draft that featured Alan Page, Bubba Smith, Gene Upshaw, Bob Griese, Willie Lanier, Mel Farr, Floyd Little and Lem Barney.

3. The Giants selected Missouri tackle Francis Peay with their first-round pick in 1966 and he played two seasons in New York. However, he blossomed into a solid offensive lineman and played eight more years in the NFL with the Green Bay Packers and the Kansas City Chiefs.

4. New York nabbed San Diego State defensive end Fred Dryer with their first-round pick in 1969 and he led the Giants in sacks for three straight years before he was dealt to the New England Patriots after butting heads with team management on multiple occasions. He never played a

down for the Patriots and was dealt to the Los Angeles Rams, where he played 10 more seasons before pursuing an active career in Hollywood.

5. The Giants struck late-round gold in 1950 with the selection of center Ray Wietecha in the 12th round. The 150th overall pick was a four-time Pro Bowl selection who was a mainstay on New York's offensive line for a decade.

6. The Giants had one of the worst drafts in their franchise history in 1971. New York selected West Texas State running back/wide receiver Rocky Thompson with the 18th overall pick. He racked up 302 combined rushing and receiving yards and three touchdowns in three seasons before getting issued his walking papers. The Giants passed on several future NFL stars including Jack Ham, Jack Youngblood, Jack Tatum, Dan Dierdorf, Julius Adams and Phil Villapiano in order to draft Thompson.

7. The Giants hit a pair of home runs in the first and fourth rounds of the 1976 NFL Draft. New York took Colorado defensive end Troy Archer in the opening round and South Carolina State linebacker Harry Carson three rounds later. Carson developed into a key team leader and future Hall of Fame player, while Archer had become one of the NFL's top defensive linemen before dying in a tragic auto accident before the 1979 season.

8. Linebacker Jessie Armstead was an eighth-round selection in 1993 whose draft stock plummeted due to a torn ACL during his sophomore season at the University of Miami.

He blossomed into one of the league's top defensive playmakers and earned five consecutive trips to the Pro Bowl with the Giants.

9. The 1975 draft will always be remembered for the player that got away and then tortured the Giants for many years as a member of the Dallas Cowboys. New York traded its first-round pick to Dallas for quarterback Craig Morton. The Cowboys selected Maryland defensive tackle and future Hall-of-Famer Randy White with the second overall pick that the Giants sent to them for Morton, who faltered with the Giants before leading the Denver Broncos to the Super Bowl.

10. The Giants were roundly booed when Morehead State quarterback Phil Simms' name was announced as the seventh overall pick in the 1979 NFL Draft. But after a tumultuous start to his career, Simms developed into a two-time Super Bowl champion who was named the Super Bowl XXI MVP.

CHAPTER 12:

THE TRADING POST

QUIZ TIME!

1. Besides Philip Rivers, how many draft picks did the Giants trade to San Diego for Eli Manning?

    a. 2
    b. 3
    c. 4
    d. 5

2. New York dealt two first-round picks and two second-round picks to the Minnesota Vikings in 1967 for quarterback Fran Tarkenton.

    a. True
    b. False

3. Which two draft picks did the Giants acquire from the New Orleans Saints in 2019 for cornerback Eli Apple?

    a. 5th and 6th
    b. 3rd and 5th
    c. 4th and 7th
    d. 2nd and 6th

4. In 1987, the Giants received which running back from the St. Louis Cardinals in exchange for second- and seventh-round draft picks?

   a. Larry Csonka
   b. Andre Brown
   c. Phillip Simms
   d. Ottis Anderson

5. When the Giants traded for veteran quarterback Y.A. Tittle in 1961, which second-year offensive lineman did the San Francisco 49ers receive as compensation?

   a. Wayne Walton
   b. Lou Cordileone
   c. Rich Buzin
   d. Francis Peay

6. When the Giants traded Homer Jones to Cleveland in 1970, which three players did New York receive from the Browns?

   a. Ron Johnson, Jim Kanicki and Wayne Meylan
   b. Bob McKay, Ben Davis and Joe Taffoni
   c. Fair Hooker, Jim Copeland and Don Gault
   d. Mike Howell, Dave Jones and Al Jenkins

7. The Houston Oilers dealt running back Rob Carpenter to the Giants during the 1981 regular season for a first-round draft pick.

   a. True
   b. False (third round)

8. The Giants committed a colossal blunder in 1974 by trading draft picks for Dallas Cowboys backup quarterback Craig Morton. Which player did Dallas draft with the second overall pick they obtained from New York in the 1975 NFL Draft?

    a. Leon Lett
    b. Harvey Martin
    c. Randy White
    d. Ed "Too Tall" Jones

9. Which veteran placekicker did New York acquire from the Kansas City Chiefs in 2007 for a conditional draft pick?

    a. Lawrence Tynes
    b. Matt Bahr
    c. Jay Feely
    d. Robbie Gould

10. The Giants were seeking to improve their running game in 2007 and traded wide receiver Tim Carter to the Cleveland Browns for which running back?

11. Dontrell Hilliard

12. Cedric Mack

13. Peyton Hillis

14. Reuben Droughns

15. New York acquired punter Brad Wing from the Pittsburgh Steelers in 2015 for a seventh-round draft pick. Which veteran punter did the Giants release on the same day of the trade?

a. Robert Malone

b. Steve Weatherford

c. Jeff Feagles

d. Brad Maynard

16. The New York Giants acquired cornerback Ross Cockrell from the Pittsburgh Steelers in 2017 for a conditional pick.

a. True

b. False

17. The Giants sent an undisclosed pick and a conditional draft pick to the Minnesota Vikings in 2010 for which two players?

a. Joe Webb and John Sullivan

b. Rhett Bomar and Jeff Dugan

c. Sage Rosenfels and Darius Reynaud

d. Patrick Ramsey and Lorenzo Booker

18. Which former first-round linebacker did the Giants receive from the Cincinnati Bengals in exchange for a fifth-round draft pick?

a. Takeo Spikes

b. Brian Simmons

c. David Pollack

d. Keith Rivers

19. New York shipped which linebacker to the Green Bay Packers in 2019 for an undisclosed draft pick?

a. B.J. Goodson

b. Greg Jones

c. Phillip Dillard

d. Clint Sintim

20. The Giants were collecting draft picks in 2019 and traded defensive tackle Damon Harrison to the Detroit Lions for a draft choice. Which draft pick did New York receive?

a. third-round

b. fifth-round

c. sixth-round

d. seventh-round

21. The Giants sent a first-round draft pick to the Los Angeles Rams in 2018 for linebacker Alec Ogletree and a 2019 seventh-round draft pick.

a. True

b. False

22. Which offensive lineman did the Minnesota Vikings acquire from the Giants in 2019 for a seventh-round draft pick?

a. Bobby Hart

b. Brandon Mosley

c. Weston Richburg

d. Brett Jones

23. To which team did the Giants trade Pro Bowl receiver Odell Beckham to in 2019?

a. Cincinnati Bengals

b. Carolina Panthers

c. Cleveland Browns

d. Detroit Lions

24. The Giants traded tight end Jeremy Shockey to the New Orleans Saints for second and fifth-round picks.

    a. True
    b. False

QUIZ ANSWERS

1. B - 3

2. A - True

3. C - 4th and 7th

4. D - Ottis Anderson

5. B - Lou Cordileone

6. A - Ron Johnson, Jim Kanicki and Wayne Meylan

7. B - False (third round)

8. C - Randy White

9. A - Lawrence Tynes

10. D - Reuben Droughns

11. B - Steve Weatherford

12. A - True

13. C - Sage Rosenfels and Darius Reynaud

14. D - Keith Rivers

15. A - B.J. Goodson

16. B - fifth-round

17. B - False

18. D - Brett Jones

19. C - Cleveland Browns

20. A – True

DID YOU KNOW?

1. The Giants acquired cornerback Dick Lynch from the Washington Redskins in 1958 for a fourth-round pick in the 1960 NFL Draft. Lynch became an All-Pro defensive back who led the league in interceptions on two different occasions and intercepted 37 passes during his nine-year pro career.

2. New York shipped a late-round draft pick to the Carolina Panthers during the 2013 season to acquire former All-Pro middle linebacker Jon Beason. The acquisition marked the first time in 27 years that the franchise had made an in-season trade. But because of injuries, Beason only played 21 games in three years with the Giants.

3. The Los Angeles Rams traded future Hall of Fame defensive end Andy Robustelli to the Giants in 1958 in a major blunder. With his wife preparing to give birth, he asked to report to training camp two weeks late. But Ram coach Sid Gillman told the defensive playmaker not to report at all if he could not arrive on time. Giants owner Wellington Mara took advantage of the situation and acquired Robustelli for a first-round pick.

4. The Giants and their crosstown rival New York Jets made a rare trade in 2019 when the G-Men acquired defensive tackle Leonard Williams for a pair of draft picks. This marked only the second time the two New York franchises

ever made a trade with each other, the first being a 1983 swap of Chris Foote for a conditional draft pick that was nullified when the Jets waived Foote later.

5. The Odell Beckham era ended in New York in 2019 when the Giants sent the ultra-talented receiver to the Cleveland Browns less than a year after inking him to a five-year, $95 million contract extension. The Browns sent a first-round pick, a third-round pick and 2017 first-rounder Jabrill Peppers to the Giants in a rare NFL blockbuster trade.

6. The Giants moved another marquee player in 2018 when defensive end Jean Pierre-Paul was dealt to the Tampa Bay Buccaneers for a 2018 third-round pick and a swap of fourth-round draft choices. New York used the third-rounder from the Buccaneers to draft North Carolina State defensive end B.J. Hill.

7. New York traded Butch Woolfolk to the Houston Oilers in 1985 for a third-round draft choice after the star running back was relegated to a backup once Joe Morris took over the starting position. The former first-round choice did catch 80 passes for 814 yards during his first season with the Oilers.

8. The New Orleans Saints acquired Jeremy Shockey from the Giants in 2009 for a second- and a fifth-round draft pick. A four-time Pro Bowl selection, Shockey was unhappy with the Giants' ground-oriented offense and wanted to play for a team that had a downfield passing offensive philosophy.

9. Tyrone Wheatley was a big, bruising 235-pound running back who led the Giants in rushing in 1997. But his lackadaisical attitude rubbed New York coaches the wrong way and he was sent packing to the Miami Dolphins for a seventh-round pick. He never played a down for the Dolphins but resurrected his career with the Oakland Raiders.

10. A sad day in the history of the Giants franchise came on April 10, 1964. The Giants traded future Hall of Fame middle linebacker Sam Huff and rookie George Seals to the Washington Redskins for defensive tackle Andy Stynchula, running back Dick James and a 1965 fifth-round pick. Besides receiving a huge pay raise in Washington, Huff became an integral part of a Redskins' defensive unit that ranked second in the NFL in 1965.

CHAPTER 13:

SUPER BOWL SPECIAL

QUIZ TIME!

1. How many NFL championships did the Giants win in the pre-Super Bowl era?

   a. 2

   b. 4

   c. 3

   d. 1

2. The New York Giants have played in a league-record 19 NFL championship title games.

   a. True

   b. False

3. The Giants were manhandled in Super Bowl XXXV in a 34-7 loss to the Baltimore Ravens. Which New York player returned a kickoff 97 yards for the Giants' only score of the game?

   a. Joe Morris

   b. Dave Meggett

c. Ron Dixon

d. Hakeem Nicks

4. New England allowed which Giants running back to score a touchdown in Super Bowl XLVI so its offense would get the ball back one more time?

a. Paul Perkins

b. Brandon Jacobs

c. Ottis Anderson

d. Ahmad Bradshaw

5. Which Giants' Super Bowl MVP became the first athlete to appear in an "I'm going to Disney World!" television ad?

a. Phil Simms

b. Jason Sehorn

c. Ottis Anderson

d. Eli Manning

6. The Patriots won the coin toss at Super Bowl XLVI to snap a long streak in the Super Bowl in which the NFC team won the coin toss. How many consecutive Super Bowls did the AFC lose the coin toss?

a. 10

b. 14

c. 12

d. 11

7. Giants quarterback Eli Manning and Patriots quarterback Tom Brady are the only two players to win three Super Bowl MVP awards.

a. True

b. False

8. Which New York defensive back intercepted a pass from John Elway on the first play of the fourth quarter in Super Bowl XXI?

a. Eli Apple

b. Kenny Phillips

c. Elvis Patterson

d. Everson Walls

9. How many countries and territories watched the Super Bowl XLII broadcast?

a. 185

b. 198

c. 216

d. 223

10. How many field goals did Giants kicker Matt Bahr make in Super Bowl XXV?

a. 2

b. 1

c. 3

d. 0

11. Tom Brady threw a critical interception deep in Giants' territory in the fourth quarter of Super Bowl XLVI. Which Giants linebacker made the key interception?

a. Gary Reasons

b. Chase Blackburn

c. Brian Kelley

d. Brad Van Pelt

12. Phil Simms earned the Super Bowl XXI MVP trophy after setting a Super Bowl record by completing 88 percent (22 of 25) passes against the Denver Broncos.

a. True

b. False

13. Which Giants receiver scored the first touchdown in Super Bowl XLVI on a short pass?

a. Hakeem Nicks

b. Amani Toomer

c. Victor Cruz

d. Stephen Baker

14. The Giants' running game help New York set a Super Bowl XXV record for time of possession. How long did New York's offense have the football in the game?

a. 40 minutes and 33 seconds

b. 38 minutes and 21 seconds

c. 42 minutes and 19 seconds

d. 37 minutes and 38 seconds

15. In Super Bowl XLII, wide receiver Plaxico Burress caught the game-winning touchdown pass with how many seconds remaining in the game?

a. 15

b. 35

c. 28

d. 49

16. Which backup quarterback, with only two starts in seven years with the franchise, led the Giants to a victory in Super Bowl XXV?

    a. Scott Brunner
    b. Dave Brown
    c. Kent Graham
    d. Jeff Hostetler

17. Super Bowl XXI marked the first time the New York Giants had reached the Super Bowl.

    a. True
    b. False

18. New York scored a safety in the second quarter of Super Bowl XXI when Denver quarterback John Elway was sacked in the end zone. Which Giants defensive end recorded the sack?

    a. Markus Kuhn
    b. Justin Tuck
    c. George Martin
    d. Leonard Marshall

19. Which New York wide receiver made the "Helmet Catch" that was the key play on the Giants game-winning touchdown drive in Super Bowl XLII?

    a. David Tyree
    b. Lionel Manuel
    c. Hakeem Nicks
    d. Victor Cruz

20. Super Bowl XXV was the first Super Bowl in NFL history in which neither team committed a turnover.

    a. True
    b. False

QUIZ ANSWERS

1. B - 4

2. A - True

3. C - Ron Dixon

4. D - Ahmad Bradshaw

5. A - Phil Simms

6. B - 14

7. B - False

8. C - Elvis Patterson

9. D - 223

10. A - 2

11. B - Chase Blackburn

12. A - True

13. C - Victor Cruz

14. A - 40 minutes and 33 seconds

15. B - 35

16. D - Jeff Hostetler

17. A - True

18. C - George Martin

19. A - David Tyree

20. A – True

DID YOU KNOW?

1. The 1934 NFL championship game between the Giants and the previously unbeaten Chicago Bears was known as "the Sneakers Game." It was played on an icy Polo Grounds in frigid conditions. New York trailed 10-3 at halftime before equipment manager Abe Cohen found nine pairs of basketball sneakers at Manhattan College. Trailing 13-3, the Giants scored 27 unanswered points in the second half to roll to a 30-13 win and claim the NFL title.

2. New York was a dominant team in the 1930 and 1940s and, during the 15-year stretch from 1933 through 1947, the Giants played in an incredible eight NFL championship games. Unfortunately, the team posted a dismal 2-6 record in NFL title games during that time.

3. The 2011 New York Giants finished the regular season 9-7 and became the first team in NFL history to reach the Super Bowl after having been outscored by opposing teams in the regular season. The Giants upset the New England Patriots in Super Bowl XLVI to claim the fourth Super Bowl win in team history.

4. The Giants played in the NFL championship game five of the six seasons from 1958 to 1963. Unfortunately, New York was 0-5 in those title games. The 1958 championship clash between the Giants and the Indianapolis Colts was a

pivotal event in the history of the NFL. Although the Colts scraped out a 23-17 victory in overtime, the game greatly enhanced the image of the league and the matchup was called "The Greatest Game Ever Played" as professional football became a major sports attraction.

5. The Giants are the only team in NFL history to have more than two second-half comebacks to win a Super Bowl and New York has accomplished the rare feat an amazing four times. The Pittsburgh Steelers, who had a pair of late come-from-behind wins in the Super Bowl, are the only other team as of 2020 to achieve the feat more than once.

6. When Giants running back Ottis Anderson was named Super Bowl XXV MVP, he was the first player to receive the new Pete Rozelle Trophy, which was named for former NFL commissioner Pete Rozelle. Anderson rushed 21 times for 102 yards and a touchdown to earn MVP honors.

7. New York set an odd record with its victory in Super Bowl XLVI, which was broadcast on NBC, by becoming the first team to win a Super Bowl on four different television networks. The Giants have won NFL titles on CBS (Super Bowl XXI), ABC (XXV), Fox (XLII)and NBC.

8. The Giants' surprising win over the undefeated New England Patriots in Super Bowl XLII is considered one of the biggest upsets in NFL history. The 12-point underdogs stunned the Patriots 17-14 in what co-owner John Mara called "the greatest victory in the history of this franchise, without question."

9. The Giants (9-7) became only the third team in NFL history to reach the Super Bowl with fewer than 10 wins since the NFL expanded to a 16-game season in 1978. Both the 1979 Los Angeles Rams and the 2008 Arizona Cardinals achieved the same feat, but New York is the only one of those three teams to win the Super Bowl after having fewer than 10 wins during the regular season.

10. Although the Giants play their home games in New Jersey, Super Bowl XXV between the New York and the Buffalo Bills was the first Super Bowl to feature two teams that represented the same state. The Giants escaped with a 20-19 victory when Scott Norwood's 47-yard field goal sailed wide right with only a few seconds left on the clock.

CONCLUSION

And there you have it! An incredible collection of Giants' history for die-hard fans who take pride in their knowledge of their favorite team. This book will both challenge and amuse New York fans of all ages.

Although some of the questions in this book are for hardcore Giants fans who are experts on the history of the four-time Super Bowl champions, there are also plenty of quiz questions for casual fanatics who just want to learn more about the colorful characters who have played for this storied franchise.

This unique book of statistics, information and little-known facts aims to inform and entertain football fans who love the game as much as their hometown team. Regardless of how well you fared on the quizzes, your knowledge about the history of the Giants will certainly be enhanced.

We hope that you have enjoyed this book and will share it with your family and friends. The Giants have a long history of Hall of Fame players who have reached the pinnacle of success on the gridiron. Find out some of the quirky stories and interesting characters as you journey back in time.

The expectations for the Giants continue to rise as the team strives for a return to prominence. And with one of the most passionate fan bases in the NFL, it is a good bet that the G-Men will be competing for more Super Bowl glory in no time at all.

Made in the USA
Middletown, DE
09 December 2020

27132769R00077